Author's Note

The purpose of this book is to help you rediscover the beauty and the magic of Christmas. This book is dedicated to my daughter Melinda, whose love of Christmas and love of people is like my own.

Visit my website at:
http://www.makingmagicstudio.com/

Christmas Star

Christmas night I saw a little star
shimmering brightly from above.
A beautiful circle of light from afar
it was softly beaming down peace and love.

It caused me to think of Christmas celebrations
from many years ago in the past.
Wonderful friends and sweet relations
brought warmth to my heart that still lasts.

Remind me often little star
to stay in touch with those I love.
Bless them with Christmas light from afar
and send them peace and love from above.

Believe in Christmas

In a cold self-serving society like ours
Peace on Earth seems like only a dream.
Yet we still believe in our God's awesome powers
He is here no matter how bad things seem.

Christmas gives us a chance to pass on
everlasting hope.
We each have been given special gifts to use
to positively affect our world
even from locations remote.
There are many tools that we can all use.

We can write and visit, phone, email and text.
That's a lot more than early Christians could do.
We just have to be willing to ask God
what to do next.
Then the hope in our hearts will become real and
brand new.

Christmas Friends

There is never a time when friends mean more
Than when Christmas comes once again.
The bells on the wreath hung on the front door
signal their arrival through snow, sleet or rain.

Their warm smiles and cheerful holiday chatter
fill the room with warmth and Christmas light.
Hot chocolate and warm apple cider shared
with laughter, expand the strength of friendship
any cold day or night.

I wouldn't give up a sweet Christmas friend
for any other treasure anywhere on Earth.
The love shared at Christmastime shouldn't end
right after we celebrate the Savior's birth.

Christmas Candle

Comforting candle bringing me delight
lighting a wonderful holiday.
It heals any pain from the lingering night
flickering hope for a happy day.

A caring gift received from far away
was sent to me with love.
It blesses my morning again today
just like healing light from above.

It's sweet aroma opens my heart
to sweet memories of Christmases past
when we were together not apart.
I am so glad our Christmas ties still last.

Christmas Light

God's boundless love and healing white light
Shines steadily through each season of the year.
However it becomes warmer just before
Christmas night.
During this time our loved ones seem
much more dear.

Getting things doesn't matter very much
when Christmas light begins shining within.
We just want to reach out and touch
other hearts that need Christmas love coming in.

God gives love at Christmas time through us
especially to those who need it so much.
Love becomes our greatest holiday focus
as God shows us hearts he wants us to touch.

Christmas Is Coming

Christmas is coming, it's almost here!
I'm ready to decorate the holiday tree.
I'll wrap up packages for loved ones dear.
Gifts will shine with bright bows from me.

Now the homemade sweets are baking nearby.
Christmas music is playing loud and clear.
My thoughts turn to holidays gone by.
I remember friends and family no longer here.

My heart goes out to those sweet lonely ones.
Some have no family near enough to share.
Christmas won't be filled with daughters and sons.
Just fear and sadness will be there.

This holiday season I'll make a new start.
My Savior will show me a special way.
This year I'm reaching out to those hurting hearts.
I will bring them love on Christmas Day.

Changing Memories

If we stopped for a minute to think about
what a long time memories about us last
If we realized we can never take out
or retrieve even a moment from the past

How would that change in some little way
how we feel about our sisters and our brothers
or relate to them on Christmas or
any other day?
How then might we share our love with others?

If we decide to make just a little change
before the next Christmas or other special day,
then we can all begin to try to rearrange
everyone's precious memories of our
Lord's birthday.

Loving You At Christmas

I love you so very much more
with your white hair and walking cane
this Christmas than on any one before.
All our holiday memories together still remain.

You made all my days better with your love
and the family of children we still share.
We have been blessed by God from above
with sweet Christmases beyond compare.

Now we pray that we have learned to share
with other families who need help this season.
Lord just show us whom and where
to give back the love you gave to us
for no reason.

Loved By A Child

If I had to name the most precious thing on Earth
it would have to be the love of a little child's heart.
"I love you" spoken by a tiny child sparks
a soul's rebirth,
spreading warmth within the coldest heart.

Healing strength is in a little child's hand.
Power resides in children's sweet laughter.
A child's love is as boundless as the mighty
ocean's sand.
Knowing this love on Earth gives a glimpse of
God's hereafter.

It's better to be loved by the heart of a child
than to amass a fortune in silver and gold.
The memory of the laughter of that child
will last a lifetime when we're old.

Little Girls at Christmas Time

Little girls at Christmas time
holding beautiful expensive dolls.
But what will a tiny poor child find
when Christmas morning calls?

God help me please to find a way
to give them a reason to smile.
Some pretty dolls I can give away
to bring them happiness for a while.

Showing the love of the Christ child
to little ones on Christmas Day
Our precious Savior meek and mild
will be honored on His birthday.

Tiny Gifts

The smallest little gift shared at Christmas time
will never escape the notice of God's eye.
Love expressed echoes through space and time.
No one can explain to us how or why.

The hearts of every one of us living here on Earth
are open books that God can see and read.
Happy loving hearts spread joy and rebirth
and desire to help other hearts
with anything they need.

Hearts connected by faith to almighty God above
will reach out with abundant gifts of caring light.
All year they send out this special kind
of care and love
with double portions to children Christmas night.

Christmas Child

Beautiful tiny infant baby
who was born on Christmas day,
You are a special little one you see
arriving on such a special day.

You will be cared for and grow strong
and learn so much right away.
Then it won't take us very long
to hear the first words you say.

Then we'll watch you learn to walk
and learn to sing your soul's own song.
Before we know it you'll be using grown-up talk
and inviting us over for Christmas laughter
and song.

God gave us a Christmas miracle on that special day.
We still thank Him every day for you.
May you be blessed the very same way
and know His love is there to bless
Christmas and every day.

Christmas's Lonely Heart

Won't you come on Christmas and visit me?
Just sit and talk for a while.
My heart has grown lonely you see.
I miss your lilting voice and broad smile.

Even though my body has grown old
my mind remains pretty bright.
Young folks live in such a hurry I'm told,
running right past family love's light.

God has blessed you with many things.
They are meant to be shared with others.
Someday you'll learn your heart only sings
when it's sweetly connected with others.

When we're gone those we have left back here
only remember the little love beams
we left in the hearts of those we held dear.
Won't you come visit me at Christmas this year?

Christmas Shopping

Christmas shopping is always fun
even with crowds of people.
Snow is quietly falling down from the
gray winter sky above.
A Christmas bell is sweetly ringing
in a nearby church steeple.
It's chiming holiday hymns that tell
about God's enduring love.

Memories from Christmases long since past
are flooding our minds
as we remember those who are no longer here.
Images come of friends and family
with packages of all kinds and
fill our hearts with love again for those so dear.

The Spirit of Christmas comes again
as on every Christmas before.
We buy presents as we always have
for all our friends and kin
and for all the family children that
our hearts most adore.
After all that Christmas shopping we know
the wrapping must begin.

Christmas Sounds

The simple sounds of Christmas
fill our hearts with joy.
We must take time to stop, be quiet and hear.
The bell ringing on a car driven by a tiny boy
or a child listening to a story about a
red-nosed reindeer.

Carolers singing familiar hymns
standing in the snow.
The music is so sweet and pure, telling
of a Savior's birth.
The memories of childhood when we
hear Santa's "HO HO HO!"
May we take the time to hear the
celebration's worth.

Our hearts never outgrow Christmas if we have
learned to share,
what we have each new year with others
just passing by.
We can always have Christmas Seasons
beyond compare,
by giving love all year long
without asking for a reason why.

Christmas Snowfall

Christmas snowflakes softly tumbling around
from a gray blue sky above
covering the Earth without a sound
delivering God's beauty and love.

High tree branches dressed in snow white silk,
Little shrubs glowing like diamonds below,
a blanket of white like frozen milk
lighting the dark with a soft white glow.

We need to just pause and really see
while time is simply standing still
incredible beauty for you and me
on Christmas our hearts to fill.

Songs From A Tree

Birds perched in the branches
of a winter white tree
God's little creatures have assembled to sing.
The chilly air is filled with their sweet melody
as perfect voices like clearest bells ring.

The power of nature's music is an awesome thing,
in an anthem led by angels from a
snow-covered tree.
The very sweetest souls hear the angels sing
when the songbirds gather in the old
winter tree.

This only occurs on Christmas Eve,
when hearts are filled with love.
It's only heard when someone does an
unselfish thing,
so pleasing to God looking down from above
that He sends songbirds and angels to sing.

Mama's Christmas Prayers

From the first Christmas with tiny you in a cradle
then a Christmas toddler giggling
over a playful kitten,
Mama's prayers were there to help enable
you little soul to grow and your brain to remember
to wear your hat and mittens.

The Christmas your first year of school
with your big girl books and knapsack,
Mama got up early to pray
that God would send an angel
to bring you safely back.

Then when teenage Christmases came so fast
and life got a little more complex,
the prayers were there to calm your fears
and problems you could not fix.

Last Christmas you were all grown up
and making it on your own.
Mama's prayers thank God for a running over cup.
She is so very proud that you are her own.

Christmas Doorway

Welcoming doorway bright with sparkling light
greeting all who glance your way.
You warm the cold of the long winter night
and welcome the morning of each brand new day.

The greens and berry wreath tied with a
perky red bow
attracts the eye of all those who might pass by.
The garland blows in the wind covered with snow.
It brings joy to hearts and a treat to every eye.

Memories of Christmas doorways from years past
come to mind as fresh as if it was seen today.
Christmas doorways give us memories that last
from childhood to our last Christmas Day.

Grandma's Special Tree

Shining through the clear cold night
I saw a most unusual tree.
Cotton wrapped branches filled with
pure white light,
shone out to welcome me.

Grandma had fashioned this special tree
for a special moment like this.
It was there where everyone could see
but I knew she had made it just for
me and Sis.

That night was so long ago in the past.
Still the memory lingers in my mind.
No matter how long my life may last
a prettier tree I will never find.

Brother's Christmas Candle

Candles shining brightly
with the holiday season's light,
with reflections of a brother
who loved the holiday season so much.
They bring back sweet memories
of a long past Christmas.
I am remembering the joy of his smile
and the warmth of his touch.

Many Christmas seasons have come
and then gone,
but never any without so many
memories of him.
Memories of Christmas celebrations
in my home with him
have never grown dim.

Thank God for the precious memories
of all the Christmases past.
I'll always light a candle
and trim a Christmas tree,
and think about my brother
for as long as my life lasts.

Christmas Angels

Angels can appear many different times and places
whispering messages and showing us signs
but we're much more likely to feel their embraces
mixed with Christmas plans and designs.

They speak very softly of sweet generous deeds
that share our love with others
especially to fill little children's needs
who are alone without fathers or mothers.

Sometimes our eyes are unable to see
but the messages are loud and clear.
God wants our hearts and hands to be
reaching out to the little ones
His heart holds so dear.

www.ingramcontent.com/pod-product-compliance
Lightning Source LLC
Chambersburg PA
CBHW042339150426
43195CB00001B/42